W9-BFA-654

FUN WITH MAP SKILLS

Pirates on the MAP

Alix Wood

PowerKiDS press

New York

3/15
J 910.4
W

Published in 2015 by Rosen Publishing
29 East 21st Street, New York, NY 10010

Copyright © 2015 by the Rosen Publishing Group, Inc.
Produced for Rosen by Alix Wood Books

Editor for Alix Wood Books: Eloise Macgregor
Designer: Alix Wood
US Editor: Joshua Shadowens
Researcher: Kevin Wood
Geography Consultant: Kerry Shepheard, B.Ed (Hons) Geography

Photo Credits: 5 bottom right, 8, 10 bottom, 19 middle and bottom,
20 bottom, 21 © Alix Wood; 12 top and bottom © Wessex Archaeology;
all other images © Shutterstock

Library of Congress Cataloging-in-Publication Data

Wood, Alix.
 Pirates on the map / by Alix Wood.
     pages cm. — (Fun with map skills)
 Includes index.
 ISBN 978-1-4777-6964-5 (library binding) — ISBN 978-1-4777-6965-2 (pbk.) —
ISBN 978-1-4777-6966-9 (6-pack)
1. Pirates—History—Juvenile literature. 2. Navigation—History—Juvenile
literature. 3. Maps—Juvenile literature. I. Title.
 G535.W69 2015
 910.4'5—dc23

                               2014000016

Manufactured in the United States of America

CPSIA Compliance Information: Batch #WS14PK9: For Further Information contact Rosen Publishing, New York, New York at 1-800-237-9932

Contents

What Is a Map?

A map is a diagram of the Earth's surface, or of part of it. Maps can be of a large area, like a **continent**, or they can be of a very small area, like your bedroom! Maps record where things are in the world. It would be very difficult to show someone where something was without a map. Maps let you know what to expect when you go to a place. They also help you know if you are going in the right direction.

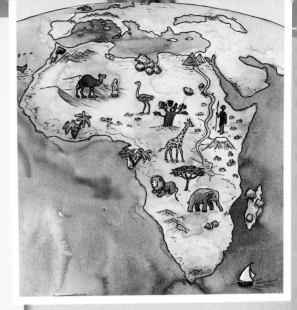

▲ Maps are used to show where things are. This map shows some of the animals that live in Africa.

No one type of map can show you everything. We need lots of different kinds of maps. A globe is shaped like a ball, which is almost the same shape as the Earth itself. Because it is the same shape, a globe can show you how the Earth really looks. It can't show you much detail, though.

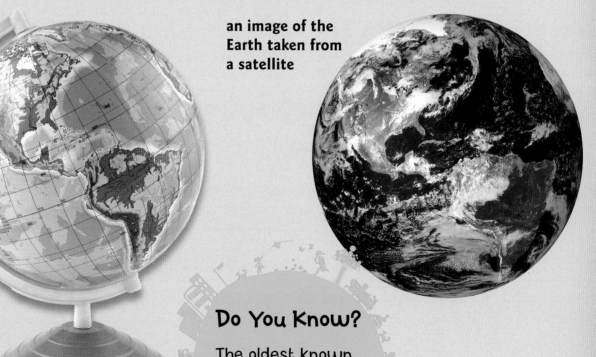

a globe

an image of the Earth taken from a satellite

Do You Know?

The oldest known globes were made in the early 1500s!

4

Maps are usually flat. People who make maps have to turn the curved Earth's surface into a flat drawing. These types of maps are called **projections**. They **distort** the shape of the continents a little.

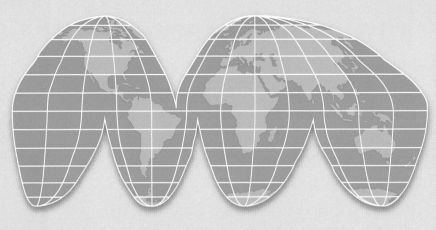

▲ This way of drawing a map is sometimes called an orange-peel projection because of its shape!

Maps can be more useful than globes. They can fold up and go in your pocket or fit on your cellphone screen. Maps can show more detail than a globe because map makers can choose smaller areas to zoom in on.

Which Map is Best?

Maps are smaller than the actual Earth, so not all the details can be shown. Map makers need to decide what they want the map to show, and what can be left out. Imagine you needed to show a pirate how to find the things below. Which type of map do you need?

1. Where is the Pacific Ocean?
2. What is the capital city of Dominica?
3. Where is the town's Jetty?

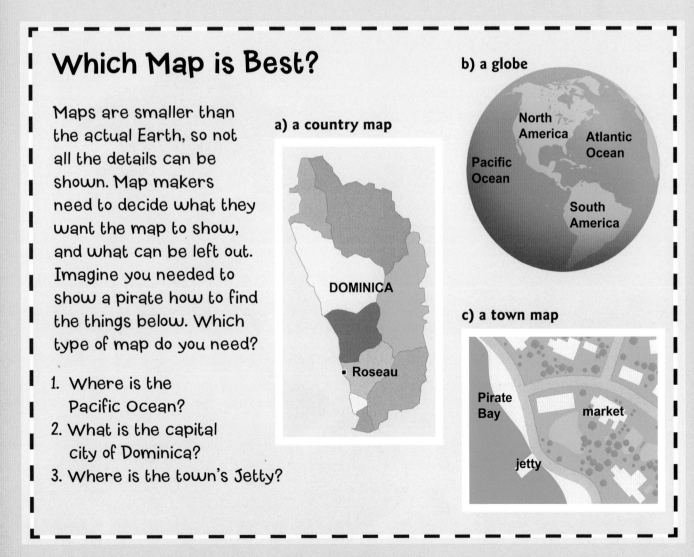

a) a country map

DOMINICA

▪ Roseau

b) a globe

North America
Atlantic Ocean
Pacific Ocean
South America

c) a town map

Pirate Bay
market
jetty

Pirates and Maps

The Golden Age of Piracy was between the 1650s to the 1730s. Pirates attacked and robbed the ships as they crossed the oceans trading goods. Pirates needed maps to find their way from place to place on land and on sea. They needed to know where the dangerous rocks and reefs were, so that they didn't damage their ships. They needed maps to work out where they were heading. They also needed to know the routes that the trading ships might take.

▲ It would be easy for a pirate ship to run aground on the rocks.

Trading ships took goods across the seas. One part of the world may have plenty of lumber, but no spices. Traders would sell their lumber, and then sail back with a ship full of things that their home country needed in exchange.

Do You Know?

Quite accurate maps had been made by the 1650s. Pirates relied on maps to **navigate** the seas, just as the traders did.

Triangular Trade Route

The map below shows the main **trade routes** in the 1600s and 1700s. The routes look a little like a triangle shape. The **key** below shows what the ships were carrying. If you were a pirate, which ships would you try and capture?

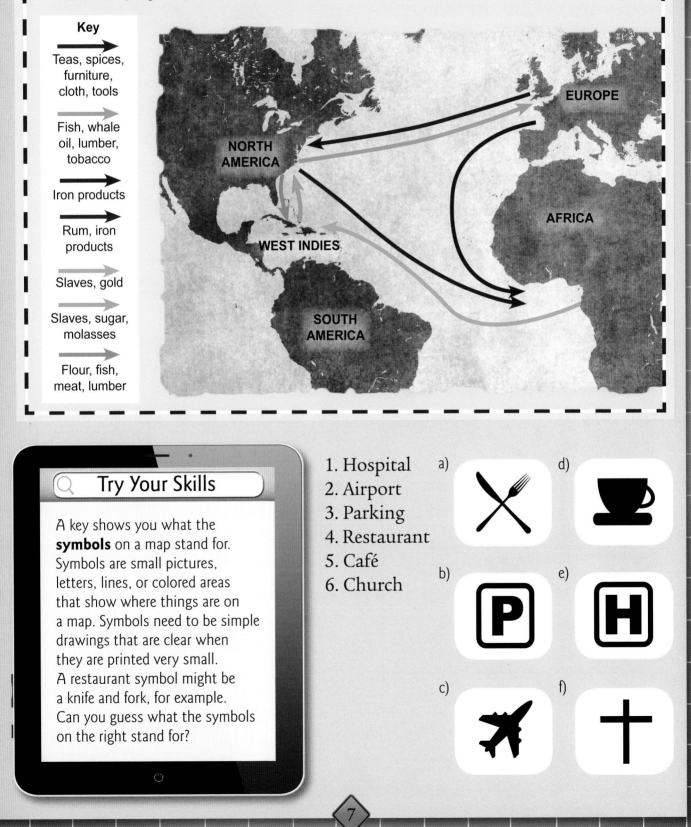

Key

→ Teas, spices, furniture, cloth, tools

→ Fish, whale oil, lumber, tobacco

→ Iron products

→ Rum, iron products

→ Slaves, gold

→ Slaves, sugar, molasses

→ Flour, fish, meat, lumber

EUROPE

NORTH AMERICA

AFRICA

WEST INDIES

SOUTH AMERICA

Try Your Skills

A key shows you what the **symbols** on a map stand for. Symbols are small pictures, letters, lines, or colored areas that show where things are on a map. Symbols need to be simple drawings that are clear when they are printed very small. A restaurant symbol might be a knife and fork, for example. Can you guess what the symbols on the right stand for?

1. Hospital
2. Airport
3. Parking
4. Restaurant
5. Café
6. Church

a)
b)
c)
d)
e)
f)

Make Your Own Map

The map on the right is a plan of a bedroom. It is drawn looking from above. This type of map is called an **aerial** view or bird's eye view. It is a great way for drawing plans. Try drawing your own map. You can use symbols for the things in your room. Make a key to show what the symbols mean.

Once you have made a plan of your bedroom, hide some treasure and mark where it is on your map with an ✘. See if a friend can follow your map and find the treasure.

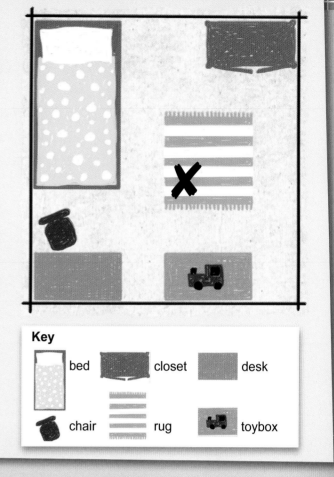

Key

bed   closet   desk

chair   rug   toybox

Try Grids

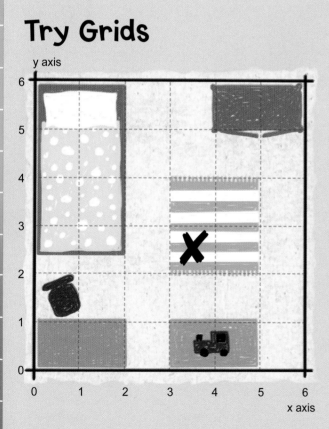

A grid helps with map reading as it divides the map into squares. You can say what square an object is in. Write down the number that goes along the grid. Then write the number that goes up and down. You can remember the order by saying "Go along the corridor and then up the stairs." You would write the grid reference for this treasure map as (3,2).

Do You Know?

You always write the number that belongs to the bottom left hand corner of the square.

Try Your Skills

Try and write the **grid reference** so that your friends can find the treasure in this picture. Write the number that goes along the bottom first, called the x **axis**. Then write the number that goes up the side, called the y axis.

Map Making!

You can make your own pirate treasure map.
To make some pirate paper you will need:

- half a cup of cold coffee or tea
- piece of white paper
- a blowdryer
- a cookie sheet

Instructions:

1. Take a piece of white paper. Rip along all the edges. Crumple the paper up tightly into a ball.
2. Flatten the paper out and put it on a cookie sheet.
3. Pour cold coffee or tea over the paper. Make sure all the paper gets covered.
4. Leave the paper in the liquid for about 5 minutes. Then drain the coffee or tea off into the sink.
5. Ask an adult to help you dry the paper gently with a hairdryer. The paper edges will start to lift away from the tray when it is dry.

Try using invisible ink to hide the location of your treasure. Paint an "x" to mark the spot in lemon juice. When it is dry ask an adult to hold the map over a candle or hot lightbulb. The invisible ink will turn brown.

9

A Real Treasure Map!

Real-life pirate "Black" Sam Bellamy's ship, the *Whydah*, sank in a storm near Cape Cod, Massachusetts on April 26, 1717. Bellamy and most of his crew drowned. The ship was full of treasure. Captain Cyprian Southack, a local **salvager** and map-maker, was sent to recover the treasure. He found part of the ship still visible above the water. Southack buried 102 of the *Whydah* crew and created a map of the site. He wrote that the treasure and the guns were buried in the sand.

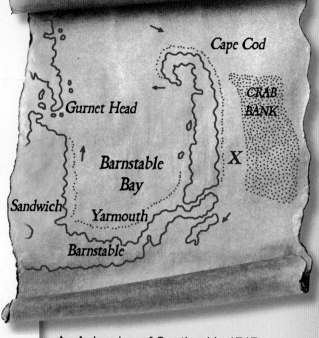

▲ A drawing of Southack's 1717 map of the *Whydah* wreck. The red X marks the spot.

Underwater explorer Barry Clifford grew up in Cape Cod. He heard tales of the *Whydah* treasure as a boy, and he dreamed of finding the wreck. Using Southack's map, after six years of searching his team found a ship's bell. On it were the words "*The Whydah Gally* 1716." The *Whydah* was found under just 14 feet (4.3 m) of water and 5 feet (1.5 m) of sand!

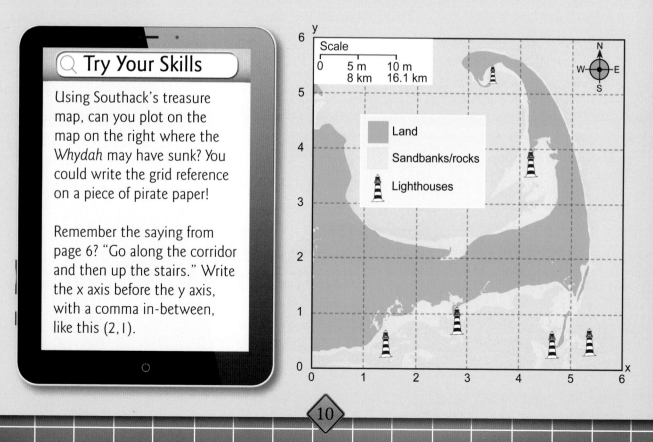

Try Your Skills

Using Southack's treasure map, can you plot on the map on the right where the *Whydah* may have sunk? You could write the grid reference on a piece of pirate paper!

Remember the saying from page 6? "Go along the corridor and then up the stairs." Write the x axis before the y axis, with a comma in-between, like this (2,1).

Plot the *Whydah*'s Treasure on the Map

Imagine you are Captain Southack and you have just arrived at the wreck of the *Whydah*. Get a piece of paper and plot where everything in the list below is. Then you and your pirate crew will be able to find it later.

1. pirate

2. barrel

3. pirate ship

4. sword

5. telescope

6. treasure chest

Write it like this;
barrel (4, 1)

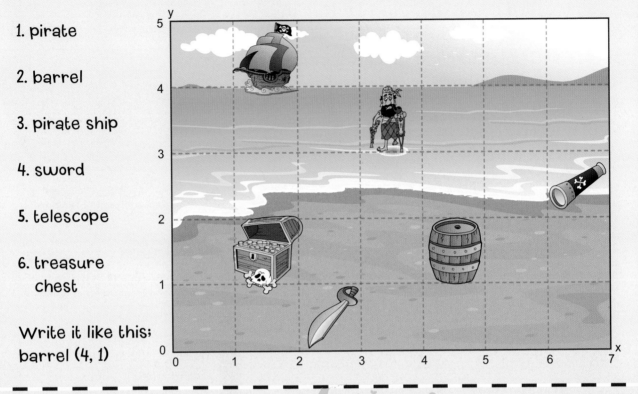

Do You Know?

This photo is of a sunset at Cape Cod. Why would there have been no point searching this beach for the wreck of the *Whydah*?

Clue: Which direction does the sun set in North America?

Mapping the Sea Bed

It is important for pirates to know how deep the sea is, to stop their ship from running aground. Measuring the depth of the ocean is called depth sounding. During the golden age of piracy, depth sounding was done using a length of rope with a lead weight tied on the end. The rope was lowered into the water, and the depth was measured by counting the knots tied at regular intervals on the rope. The measurement between the knots was called a fathom.

A fathom was measured as the distance between fingertip to fingertip with outstretched arms. As arm lengths varied, a fathom was later standarized to be 6 feet (1.83 m). Sailors would tie different markers at intervals along the line that could either be seen by day or could be felt with the hands at night. Some markers would be leather and some would be cloth, so sailors could feel the difference at night.

🔍 Try Your Skills

Would you have made a good depth sounder? Measure the distance between your outstretched arms. Is it a fathom or less? Usually the distance from a person's fingertips to fingertips is the same measurement as a person's height.

▲ What height would you need to be to have an arm span of a fathom?

12

Swing the lead

You are on a pirate ship heading towards an island. Each route shows the depth in fathoms along the way. A fathom is 6 feet (1.83 m). The bottom of your boat lies 6 feet (1.83 m) below the water. Should you take route A, B, or C to be sure your route will be deep enough?

To work out what the **terrain** was like beneath a ship, the crew put meat fat in the hole at the bottom of the lead weight. The sticky fat would bring up sand, pebbles, clay, or shells from the sea bed. If it came up clean, it meant the bottom was rock.

Do You Know?

Different harbors have different kinds of soil. Pirates could use this knowledge to help work out their location.

Shell Point

Pebble Beach

Sandy Shores

Look at the bottom of the lead weight. Which beach do you think the pirates are the closest to?

Using a Compass

Pirates would have used a compass to help them navigate. The Earth is like a giant magnet. The north and south poles are magnetic. A compass has a magnetic needle which will always point to the **north magnetic pole**. The compass has a drawing of a **compass rose** on it. The compass rose shows the points of the compass. The four main **cardinal directions** are north, south, east, and west.

Maps will usually have a drawing of a compass rose on them. On most maps north points toward the top of the map. If you go clockwise around the compass the main points are north, then east, then south, and finally west. Some compass roses have the directions written in degrees (°), too. A circle is made up of 360°. Starting with north as 0°, look around the circle in a clockwise direction and see what number is used for each compass point.

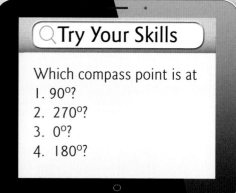

Try Your Skills

Which compass point is at
1. 90°?
2. 270°?
3. 0°?
4. 180°?

Do You Know?

An easy way to remember the points of the compass is to say this phrase: **Never Eat Slimy Worms.**

14

Pirate Pete is lost.
Help him decide if he
should go north, south,
east, or west.

1. Which direction is his ship?
2. Which direction is the treasure?
3. Which direction is the barrel?
4. Which direction is the small island?

Pirate Hide-Outs

Even the most skilled sailors couldn't stay at sea forever. Pirates needed safe places to come ashore. They needed shelter from bad weather, and somewhere to hide from their enemies. Finding a small island in a big ocean was not easy. Pirates had to be confident they were sailing in the right direction when all they could see was water!

Sometimes north, south, east, and west aren't precise enough. You need other directions in-between to make your map reading and navigating more accurate. **Intermediate directions** are halfway between the four cardinal directions. The intermediate directions are northeast, northwest, southeast, and southwest. Just as north is shortened to "N" on maps, intermediate directions' names are shortened too.

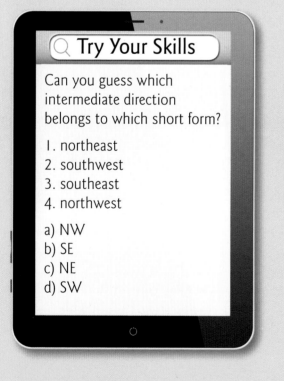

Try Your Skills

Can you guess which intermediate direction belongs to which short form?

1. northeast
2. southwest
3. southeast
4. northwest

a) NW
b) SE
c) NE
d) SW

▲ This compass rose shows you where the intermediate directions are.

Use Your Compass To Find the Hide-Outs

Pirates had a few safe places to hide in the Caribbean. Nassau in the Bahamas was surrounded by tiny islands, **shoals**, and **reefs** which helped the pirates to hide. The island of Tortuga in Haiti hired pirates to help defend the island and was a perfect pirate base. Port Royal in Jamaica was a large town and also a popular pirate haunt. The Isla de la Juventud in Cuba used to be called Treasure Island! It has a long pirate history.

Use compass bearings to get the pirates to a safe hide-out!

1. What direction is Tortuga from Nassau?
2. What direction is Isla de la Juventud from Nassau?
3. What direction is Isla de la Juventud from Port Royal?
4. What direction is Tortuga from Port Royal?

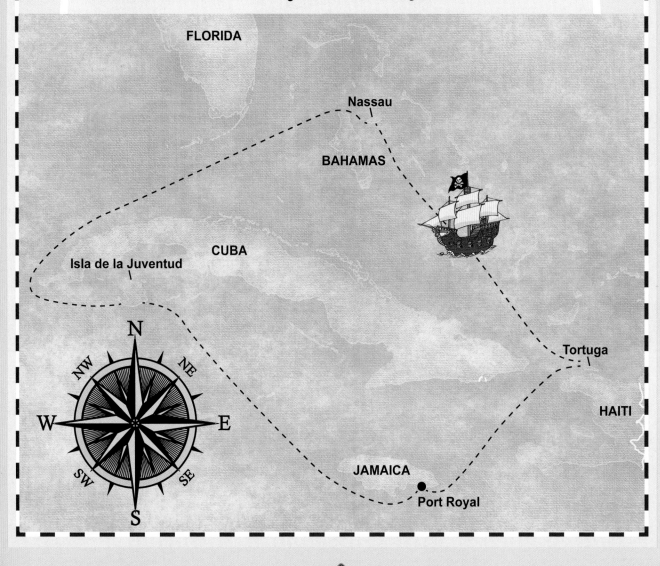

How High Are the Mountains?

The world is not flat. There are mountains and valleys. Pirates may need to know the height of the land. If there was a range of mountains on an island, pirates would prefer to go around the mountains rather than over them. There are a few different ways of showing **physical features** on a map. You can draw a symbol like on the map below, to show where mountains are. You won't know how tall they are though.

There is a great way of accurately showing how high the land is on a map. A relief map shows the different heights of land in different colors. The lowest land is usually dark and the tallest points are paler. The maps are often colored realistically, like in the map below. The **plains** will be green and the mountains will be brown. The deep sea will be dark blue and the shallow sea is light blue.

▼ The Earth and the oceans both have valleys and mountains. Pirates found it useful to have a map of the land and the sea bed.

Use a Relief Map to Pick a Pirate Look-Out Spot

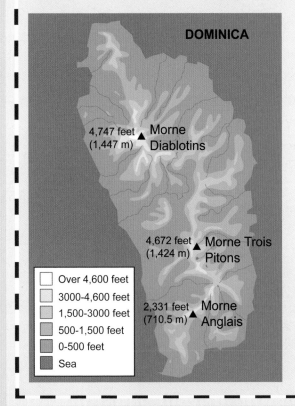

DOMINICA

4,747 feet (1,447 m) ▲ Morne Diablotins

4,672 feet (1,424 m) ▲ Morne Trois Pitons

2,331 feet (710.5 m) ▲ Morne Anglais

- ☐ Over 4,600 feet
- ☐ 3000-4,600 feet
- ☐ 1,500-3000 feet
- ☐ 500-1,500 feet
- ☐ 0-500 feet
- ☐ Sea

Relief maps show how far above sea level the land is. In this map of Dominica the flat plains are colored in green. The higher the land is, the paler shade of green that is used. The height of the mountain is often written next to it, too. The island of Dominica is in the Caribbean. It was a favorite hideout for pirates! Spanish **galleons** full of gold would often sail by.

1. If you were a pirate and wanted to watch for ships far out at sea, which mountain would you choose to stand on to get the best view?

   a) Morne Diablotins b) Morne Trois Pitons
   c) Morne Anglais

Here are two maps of Pirate Mountain. The first is a **profile map** that shows the mountain from the side. The second map shows the same mountain from above.

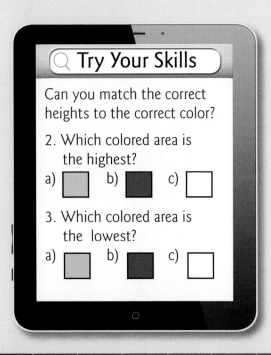

Try Your Skills

Can you match the correct heights to the correct color?

2. Which colored area is the highest?

   a) ☐ b) ☐ c) ☐

3. Which colored area is the lowest?

   a) ☐ b) ☐ c) ☐

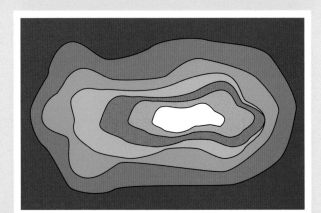

Escape to Skull Mountain

Pirates needed places to stash their treasure and meet fellow pirates. They wanted a place that was easy to find and easy to describe. Skull Mountain would have been a great pirate meeting place. Pirates could draw a symbol of the mountain so other pirates could spot it if they sailed past. But what if the pirates were approaching by land, from the other side of the mountain? They wouldn't see the skull face from that side.

Contour maps show the height of land just like relief maps do. Contour maps use lines instead of colored areas. The lines link areas that are the same height.

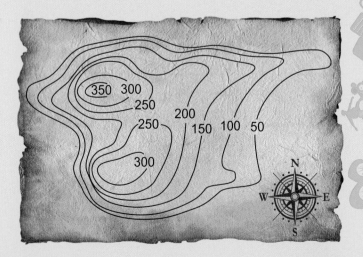

Do You Know?

If contour lines are close together, the slope is steep. If they are far apart, the slope is shallow. Which side of the mountain pictured left isn't as steep as the others? North, south, east, or west?

Help the Pirates Find Skull Mountain!

The pirates are meeting at Skull Mountain today. Can you tell which of these mountains is which from their contour maps? Look at the profile maps on the left and see if you can match them to the correct contour maps on the right.

Profile Maps

1.

Skull Mountain

2.

Treasure Chest Mountain

3.

Pointy Peak

Contour Maps

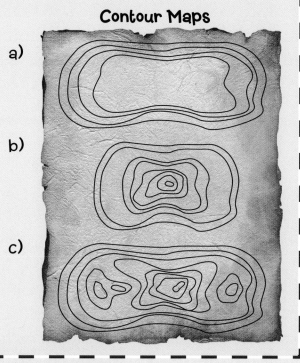

a)

b)

c)

🔍 Try Your Skills – Draw A Contour Map

You will need: clay, wire, a sheet of paper, a toothpick, and a pencil.

Fold the paper in half lengthways and widthways. Open out the paper and mark the top fold as north. Model a mountain out of the clay. Make a dot with a toothpick at the top of the mountain. Mark the direction of north on top with a line. Place the mountain on the paper with north lined up and the dot over the center fold. Draw around the base of the mountain. Next, mark the sides of the mountain so it is divided into four equal parts. Carefully slice through the bottom quarter. Line up the new shorter mountain on the paper and trace around it. Continue doing this until you have traced around all three slices. You should now have a contour map of your clay mountain!

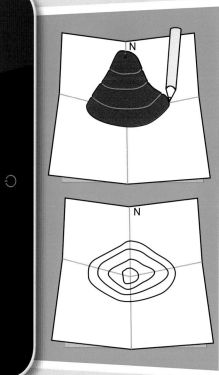

What's the Scale?

On a map things need to be shown smaller than actual size. This shrinking is called **scale**. Different scales show different levels of detail. A small scale map shows a large area, so there isn't much detail. A large scale map zooms right in on an area and has much more detail. A medium scale map is between the two.

A scale on a map tells you how the map compares with real life. The scale is written as a **ratio**. The scale 1:10 means that one unit of measurement on the map is the same as 10 units of measurement in real life. Maps often show a **linear scale**, too. The line shows how many miles (km) are represented by a smaller measurement, such as an inch (cm).

Do You Know?

Small scale maps don't usually have a linear scale on them. Why do you think that is?

Look at these maps of the Gambia. The small island in the river Gambia in the medium scale map below was the scene of a famous pirate trick. A castle used for slave trading was built on the island.

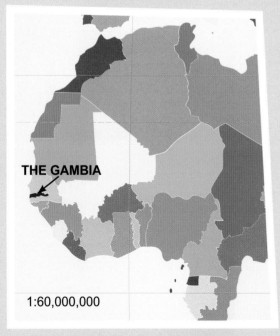

THE GAMBIA

1:60,000,000

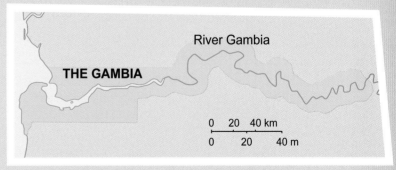

THE GAMBIA

River Gambia

| 0 | 20 | 40 km |
| 0 | 20 | 40 m |

▲ This is a small scale map of the west coast of Africa. The map scale is 1:60,000,000. The country of the Gambia is very small on this map.

▲ This is a medium scale map. The area in green is the Gambia. This map has a linear scale. You can use the linear scale to measure distance.

22

Real-life pirate Howell Davis preferred using trickery than violence. In 1718, Captain Davis decided to attack a fort on the river Gambia. Davis pretended to be a wealthy merchant wanting to buy slaves. He befriended the castle commander, who invited him to a welcoming dinner.

At the dinner Davis and his men put themselves between the castle guards and their weapons which were hanging on the walls. Then Davis pulled a pistol on the commander. Davis' men took the castle without firing a shot! The pirates locked up the soldiers and drank all the alcohol in the castle. They also fired the fort's cannons to entertain themselves, and made off with 2,000 pounds (907 kg) of treasure!

Help Captain Davis Sack Gambia Castle

How far away are the weapons and treasure from Captain Davis on this large scale map? Use a piece of cotton to measure the distance with. Measure from the middle of each symbol. The scale shows 1 cm is equal to 5 meters, and that 1 inch is 13.6 yards.

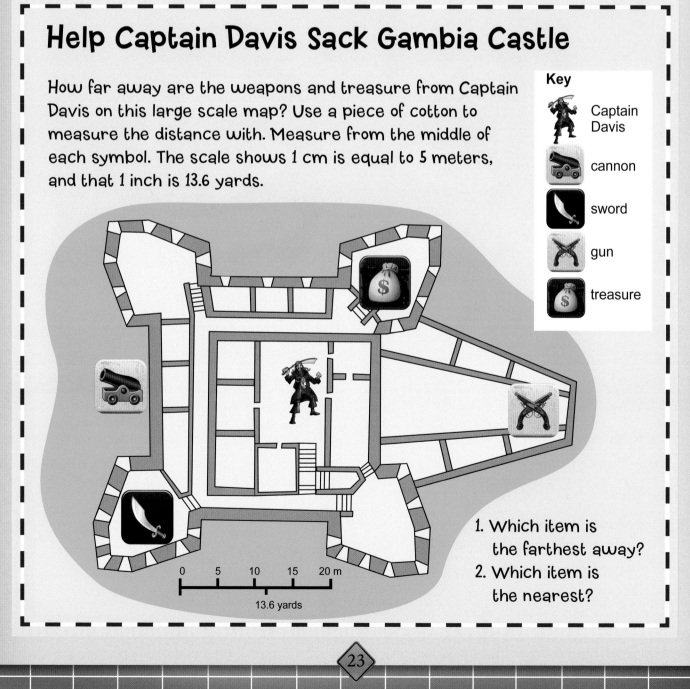

Key

Captain Davis

cannon

sword

gun

treasure

0   5   10   15   20 m

13.6 yards

1. Which item is the farthest away?
2. Which item is the nearest?

Measuring Distance

Pirates needed to know how far their sailing trips around the world would be. This would help them work out how long the trip would take, and how much food they would need. Using a piece of thread, measure each of these journeys by placing the thread along the line and marking the beginning and end of the journey. Then measure the journey's length of thread along a ruler. Can you answer the questions below?

ENGLAND

CALIFORNIA

FLORIDA

SPAIN

CUBA

THE GAMBIA

Do You Know?

Pirates called expert navigators "sea artists!" Navigators were important crew members.

🔍 Try Your Skills

1. Which journey is the longest?

a) England to Florida?
b) Spain to Cuba?
c) The Gambia to California?

2. Which journey is the shortest?

a) England to Florida?
b) Spain to Cuba?
c) The Gambia to California?

Ten Paces North

Pirate maps used everyday things to measure distance. Treasure maps would often be measured out in footsteps and compass directions. Can you follow the instructions on this map to walk to the correct place to dig for the treasure?

Trace this footprint to use as your measure.

1. Start at the middle of the red X.
2. Walk 2 steps east.
3. Turn and walk 4 steps northeast.
4. Walk 4 steps northwest.
5. Walk one step east.
6. The treasure is buried under your feet.

Where are you?

Longitude and Latitude

Like grid lines, lines of longitude and latitude help pirates find places on maps. Lines of longitude go from the top to the bottom of a globe. Lines of latitude go across the globe. Each line is numbered. Places can be located on a globe by a number. The north or south position on the lines of latitude is always written first, followed by the east or west position on the lines of longitude. A way to remember is by saying "first, go up or down the rungs of a ladder-tude."

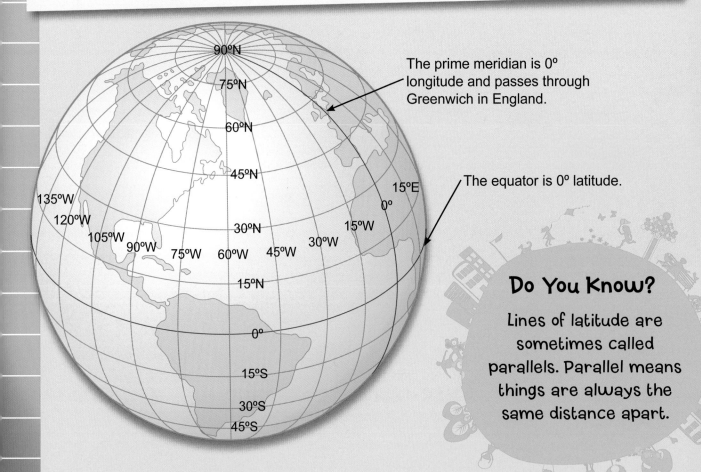

The prime meridian is 0° longitude and passes through Greenwich in England.

The equator is 0° latitude.

Do You Know?

Lines of latitude are sometimes called parallels. Parallel means things are always the same distance apart.

The prime meridian is 0° longitude. Any lines of longitude heading west from the prime meridian are written with a W after them. Any lines of longitude heading east have a E after them. East and west meet at 180°. This is opposite the prime meridian line on a globe.

The equator is 0° latitude. Lines of latitude north or south of the equator have an S or an N after them.

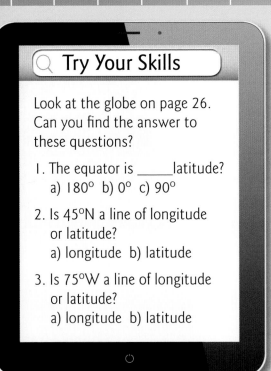

Try Your Skills

Look at the globe on page 26. Can you find the answer to these questions?

1. The equator is _____ latitude?
   a) 180° b) 0° c) 90°

2. Is 45°N a line of longitude or latitude?
   a) longitude b) latitude

3. Is 75°W a line of longitude or latitude?
   a) longitude b) latitude

Hemispheres

The equator separates the Earth into two hemispheres. The northern hemisphere is above the equator and the southern hemisphere is below. The prime meridian separates the Earth into the western and eastern hemispheres.

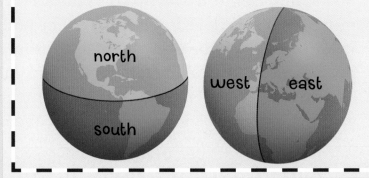

north

south

west | east

Pirate Bill has forgotten to put on the east and west on his treasure map longitude lines! Can you help the pirates? Be careful. This map symbol means certain death!

1. Treasure Island is at 60°
   a) west b) east
2. Blackbeard's ship is at 150°
   a) west b) east
3. A bag of gold is at 15°
   a) west b) east

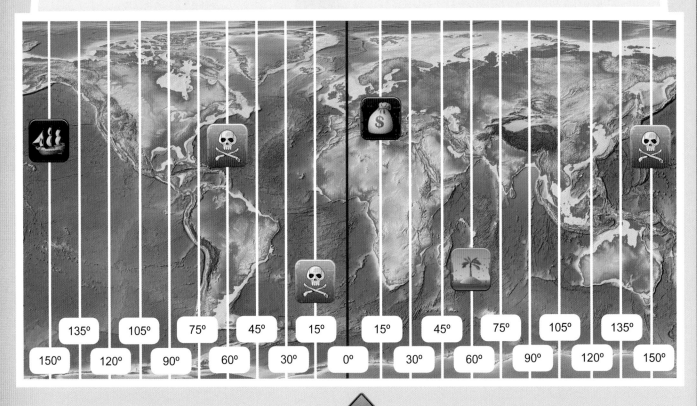

135° 105° 75° 45° 15° 15° 45° 75° 105° 135°

150° 120° 90° 60° 30° 0° 30° 60° 90° 120° 150°

Crossing the Line

Sailors have a traditional ceremony for anyone who crosses the equator for the first time on a voyage. Sailors who have never crossed the equator before are called "slimy pollywogs." Usually one of the officers dresses up as King Neptune and holds a court. Pollywogs must pay respect to King Neptune. The pollywogs are made to suffer some unpleasant but funny tricks. After the ceremony, the "slimy pollywogs" become "trusty shellbacks." Some modern ships hoist the pirate flag, the Jolly Roger, when King Neptune is aboard!

▲ The pirate flag, the Jolly Roger.

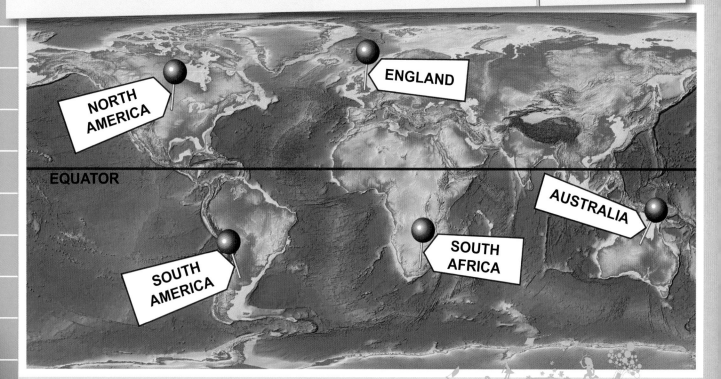

NORTH AMERICA

ENGLAND

EQUATOR

SOUTH AMERICA

SOUTH AFRICA

AUSTRALIA

If pirates set sail on the voyages below, would they cross the equator?

1. North America to England?
2. South Africa to North America?
3. Australia to South America?
4. England to South Africa?

Do You Know?

Places on the equator have twelve hours of day and twelve hours of night all year. Places north or south of the equator have longer or shorter days depending on the seasons.

28

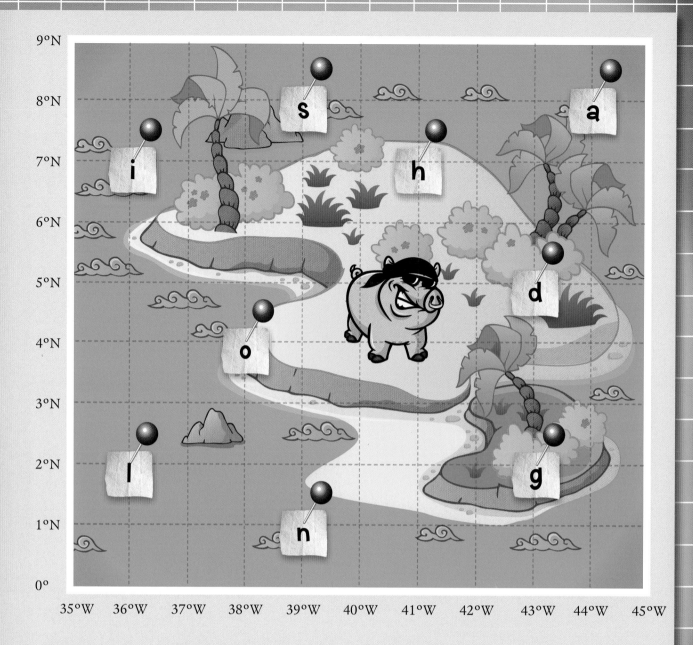

9°N
8°N — s — a
7°N — i — h
6°N
5°N — d
4°N — o
3°N
2°N — l — g
1°N — n
0°

35°W 36°W 37°W 38°W 39°W 40°W 41°W 42°W 43°W 44°W 45°W

Help the Pirates Find the Unknown Island

Pirate Billy pinned the mystery island's name on this map. All the pirates have to do is put the letters in the right order. Can you help? Find the right letter for each box using longitude and latitude. The letters will spell out the name of the island.

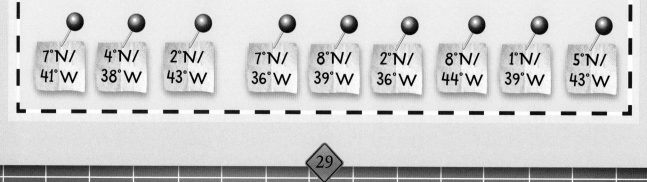

7°N/ 41°W   4°N/ 38°W   2°N/ 43°W   7°N/ 36°W   8°N/ 39°W   2°N/ 36°W   8°N/ 44°W   1°N/ 39°W   5°N/ 43°W

Glossary

aerial (EHR-ee-ul)
Taken from the air, such as a
photograph from above.

axis (AK-sus)
A number line (as an x-axis or a y-axis)
along which coordinates are measured.

cardinal directions
(KAHRD-nul dih-REK-shunz)
One of the four principal points of
the compass: north, south, east, west.

compass rose (KUM-pus ROHZ)
A drawing on a map which
shows directions.

continent (KON-tuh-nent)
One of the great divisions of land
(as North America, South America,
Europe, Asia, Africa, Australia, or
Antarctica) on the globe.

contour (KON-toor)
A line (as on a map) connecting the
points that have the same elevation
on a land surface.

distort (dih-STORT)
To twist out of a natural, normal,
or original shape or condition.

galleons (GA-lee-unz)
Large sailing ships with square sails
used from the 1400s to the 1700s
especially by the Spanish.

grid reference (GRID REH-frens)
A point on a map defined by two sets
of numbers or letters.

intermediate direction
(in-ter-MEE-dee-et dih-REK-shun)
Northeast, northwest, southeast,
or southwest.

key (KEE)
A map legend.

linear scale (LIH-nee-er SKAYL)
A scale resembling a line.

navigate (NA-vuh-gayt)
To direct one's course in a ship
or aircraft.

north magnetic pole
(NORTH mag-NEH-tik POHL)
The direction of the Earth's magnetic
pole, to which the north-seeking pole
of a magnetic needle points when free
from local magnetic influence.

physical features
(FIH-zih-kul FEE-churz)
Landforms such as deserts,
mountains, and plains.

plains (PLAYNZ)
Broad areas of level or rolling
treeless country.

profile map (PROH-fel MAP)
A map that shows the cross section of a land surface.

projections (pruh-JEK-shunz)
A method of showing a curved surface (as the Earth) on a flat one (as a map).

ratio (RAY-shoh)
The relationship in quantity, amount, or size between two or more things.

reefs (REEFS)
Chain of rocks or ridges of sand at or near the surface of water.

salvager (SAL-vij-er)
A person who rescues or saves especially from wreckage or ruin.

shoals (SHOHLZ)
Sandbanks or sandbars just below the surface of the water.

symbols (SIM-bulz)
Drawings that stand for real things.

terrain (tuh-RAYN)
The surface features of an area of land.

trade routes (TRAYD ROOTS)
A route used by traveling traders or merchant ships.

Read More

Bergin, Mark. *Pirates*. New York: Windmill Books, 2012.

Macdonald, Fiona. *Nasty Pirates*. New York: Gareth Stevens, 2011.

Quinlan, Julia J. *How to Draw a Map*. New York: PowerKids Press, 2012.

Index

B
Bellamy, Sam 10, 11

C
cardinal directions 14, 15
compass directions 14, 15
compasses 14
compass roses 14
contour lines 20
contour maps 20, 21

D
depth sounding 12, 13

E
equator 26, 27, 28

F
fathoms 12, 13

G
globes 4
grid references 8, 9, 10
grids 8, 9

H
hemispheres 27

I
intermediate directions 16, 17
invisible ink 9

K
keys 7

L
latitude 26, 27
linear scales 22
longitude 26, 27

M
map making 8, 9
measuring distances 23, 24, 25

P
prime meridian 26, 27
profile maps 19, 21
projections 5

R
ratios 22
relief maps 18, 19

S
scale 22, 23
symbols 7

W
Whydah, The 10, 11

- -

Answers

page 5
1 b; 2 a; 3 c

page 7
1 e; 2 c; 3 b; 4 a; 5 d; 6 f

page 9
The treasure is at (3, 2).

page 10
The *Whydah* probably sunk at (5, 2).

page 11
1. (3, 3); 2. (4, 1); 3. (1, 4); 4. (2, 0); 5. (6, 2); 6. (1, 1)
The Sun sets in the west. On an east-facing beach the setting sun would not be over the ocean.

page 12
6 feet (1.83 m) tall.

page 13
Take route A.
The pirates are at Pebble Beach.

page 14
1 east; 2 west; 3 north; 4 south

page 15
1 north; 2 east; 3 west; 4 south

page 16 1 c; 2 d; 3 b; 4 a

page 17
1 southeast; 2 southwest; 3 northwest; 4 northeast

page 19
1 a; 2 c; 3 b

page 20
east

page 21
1 c; 2 a; 3 b

page 23
1 gun; 2 treasure

page 24
1 c; 2 a

page 25
The west side of the lake.

page 27
Try Your Skills 1 b; 2 b; 3 a
Pirate Billy's Map
1 b; 2 a; 3 b

page 28
1. no; 2. yes; 3. no; 4. yes

page 29 Hog Island

A